P U B W
FOR THE

Essex

Norman Skinner

COUNTRYSIDE BOOKS
NEWBURY, BERKSHIRE

COUNTRYSIDE BOOKS
3 Catherine Road
Newbury, Berkshire

ISBN 1 85306 286 3

Designed by Mon Mohan
Cover illustration by Colin Doggett
Photographs and maps by the author

Produced through MRM Associates Ltd., Reading
Typeset by Paragon Typesetters, Clwyd
Printed and bound by Woolnough Bookbinders, Wellingborough

Contents

Area map showing locations of the walks.

Introduction

In today's world there are few activities which can be enjoyed by all members of the family at the same time. One of these is walking in the countryside. The walks described in this book are from 2 to 3¾ miles in length, and include walks on the coast, through forests, and in other parts of the lovely Essex countryside. Each walk is circular, starting from a good pub where food and drink can be served for all the family. All the pubs in this book welcome those aged under 14 with their parents to a section of the pub which is specifically for that purpose – usually termed a 'children's room' or a 'family room'.

The walks have been spread around the county so I hope that as well as some not too far from home you will be tempted to travel to parts of Essex which perhaps may have been previously unknown to you. The county is surprisingly varied in its landscape, and quite short walks can show this diversity. Each area in this book has a charm well worth savouring and I trust that readers will want to visit all the pubs and complete all the walks. Any time of the year is right, although walking is different in each season (one of the joys of walking in the countryside).

You should wrap up well in the cold weather, wear a hat when it's hot and sunny, and if it has been wet, choose footwear that can cope with mud, and carry waterproofs. In these circumstances do remember to cover muddy boots or take them off, where necessary, if you want to go in the pub after the walk.

I hope that the directions given will enable you to find your way with the help of the sketch maps. I suggest that you carry the appropriate OS Landranger map as this will be helpful. All but four of the walks are contained on maps 167 or 168, and most public libraries will be able to lend you the ones you need.

I would like to express gratitude to my wife Ann. She has produced the walk maps and photographs of all the pubs, as well as exploring many of the walks with me in the course of preparing the text. I do hope that this book will provide hours of pleasure for readers of all ages.

Norman Skinner
spring 1994

Publisher's Note

We hope that you obtain considerable enjoyment from this book; great care has been taken in its preparation. However, changes of landlord and actual closures are sadly not uncommon. Likewise, although at the time of publication all routes followed public rights of way or well-established permitted paths, diversion orders can be made and permissions withdrawn.

We cannot accept responsibility for any inaccuracies, but we are anxious that all details covering both pubs and walks are kept up to date, and would therefore welcome information from readers which would be relevant to future editions.

Dedicated to so many of my relatives who have helped me discover the pubs with a welcome for the family, as well as encouraging me to find the paths leading to their doors.

1 Epping Forest
The Owl

High Beach is a beautiful part of Epping Forest, and is probably the jewel in its crown. Tennyson must have agreed as he lived here from 1837 to 1840 to be nearer London. On winter days he would skate on a pond in the park and he loved to visit his friends in town. Returning in the evening he would notice 'the light of London flaring like a dreary dawn'. The poet loved walking, and undoubtedly he loved to walk in the forest.

The great forest of Epping gives to a piece of England that might have become a suburb of London an air of rural serenity. Once the forest covered the land all the way to Colchester. As time passed the Essex Forest became Waltham Forest, Waltham Forest became Epping Forest, and this was in danger when, in the late 19th century, the City of London saved the forest from perishing, so preserving for all time its 5,500 acres of land, seven miles long as one of the great treasures in the county. It was of course a royal forest, one of the hunting grounds for the kings and queens of England. Queen Elizabeth I's Hunting

Lodge at Chingford is a Tudor timber-framed 'standing' from which spectactors could follow the progress of the chase.

'There will always be an England' the song says, so what were the thoughts of regular visitors to the Owl at Lippits Hill when in the early '70s the old thatched building was threatened with demolition? As it was a listed building they must have been shocked when McMullen's brewery and the local authority agreed on the danger of trying to maintain it. What a pity! Nevertheless the new building has settled down to be a very popular place, especially in the summer, and it occupies the old site with dignity. The many windows in both bars give lovely views of the glorious woodland.

Opening hours are from 11 am to 2.30 pm and 6 pm to 11 pm Monday to Saturdays (12 noon to 3 pm and 7 pm to 10.30 pm Sundays). The real ales are McMullen's Original AK and Country Bitter plus a guest beer. A good selection of traditional pub grub, including basket meals, is offered, backed up by a variety of Mexican food. There is a children's room and a large garden looks over the forest. Part of the terrace is covered so there is plenty of opportunity to be outdoors for your visit to Epping Forest. Throughout the summer a large barbecue is operated in the garden – hugely popular on Sundays.

Telephone: 081-502 0663.

How to get there: Between Epping and Chingford the A104 runs through Epping Forest. At the Robin Hood roundabout take the exit signposted to High Beach. Just past High Beach church the road left is signposted to Lippits Hill and you will soon arrive at the Owl.

Parking: At the Owl there are two car parks. Please ask the manager for permission to park before you leave your car to set out on the walk.

Length of the walk: 3 miles. Map: OS Landranger 177 East London Area (inn GR 398970).

Lippits Hill, just out of the forest, offers glorious views and it is from here that our walk starts. It climbs to the conservation centre at High Beach, then follows a forest path, reaching more open ground at Fairmead Bottom. From

9

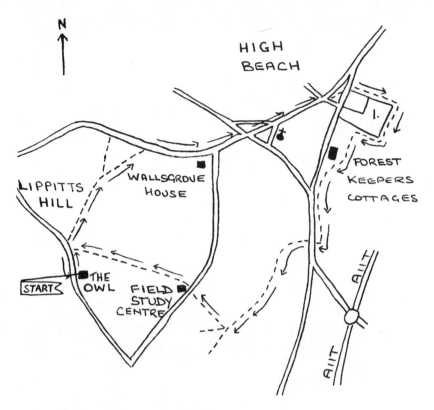

N

HIGH
BEACH

I.

LIPPITTS
HILL

WALLSGROVE
HOUSE

FOREST
KEEPERS
COTTAGES

START

THE
OWL

FIELD
STUDY
CENTRE

I. = EPPING FOREST
CONSERVATION CENTRE

NOT TO SCALE

here you turn to the Sun Trap Field Study Centre and return to the Owl by a pretty path.

The Walk

The Owl, in its lovely setting on Lippits Hill, has an unlikely neighbour: of all things, a police firearms training centre. Leave the pub and turn right along the road. Pass a footpath sign on your right. After 40 yards turn right at a bridleway sign beside a barn. Soon turn right again along a muddy track and left to a gate. Continue straight across a field in the line of the telegraph poles to reach a metal gate. Through the gate you enter Pepper Alley, a hedged track which can be muddy. Conditions underfoot improve as you climb and after passing some garages a dimpled concrete surface provides an easy walk to reach a road. Turn right along the road to Wallsgrove House at a T-junction. Continue straight on by a road signposted to High Beach. Pass the Kings Oak Pub and go to the conservation centre next door, which is well worth a visit. The walk continues along the northern fence of the centre, with the fence on your right. At the fence corner, turn right, still following the fence. At the next corner follow the path to the south-west. You should arrive at a road between a road junction on your right and another junction on your left with a tea-hut. Across the road there is a solid track marked 'emergency access'. Follow this track which will lead you past Hill Wood to an open area not far from Fairmead Bottom. Here the track turns sharp right over a stream. Do not turn left with the track but continue to walk north-west along a ride. Soon some houses come into view, and the right hand one is the Sun Trap Field Studies Centre. From here parties of schoolchildren are given conducted tours of the forest.

Cross the road and enter a short track to the right of the centre. Go over a stile and walk straight on with a wall and later a hedge on your left. Cross two more stiles. The path passes by the side of a mobile home park (there are magnificent views to the right). A final stile takes you out to the road. Turn left and walk a few yards back to the Owl.

Fiddlers Hamlet
The Merry Fiddlers

Times have certainly changed in the last 25 years for this little place, consisting of no more than a pub, a school, a farm and a handful of houses tucked away off the road between Epping and Theydon Mount. Then first came the M11, to within 300 yards. Next was the M25 and an interchange less than ¾ mile off. Miraculously the hamlet and the surrounding countryside retain a charm well apparent to those who will venture forth on foot. Was the pub named after the place or the place after the pub? I suspect the latter, but I am not certain.

The Merry Fiddlers is yet another example of the improvements accruing from a more liberal beer policy, and a determination to satisfy a wider variety of food tastes. The pub is in fact over 300 years old and neatly positioned 1¼ miles from Epping station but well into the countryside. Real ales are Adnams, Webster's Yorkshire Bitter and Burton Ale, with Scrumpy Jack cider also available. The food is wholesome and unpretentious. Steak and kidney pie and filled jacket potatoes are amongst the dishes on offer. Part of the attraction for the family is a well-established room which accommodates children, with independent access from the car park, and entrance to the toilets without intrusion into the bar. These facilities are available to all ages at lunchtime, but are restricted to eight years and over on Sunday to Friday evenings, and to twelve years and over on Saturday evenings. The pub hours are 11.30 am to 2.30 pm lunchtimes (Sundays 12 noon to 3 pm) and 5.30 pm to 11 pm evenings (Sundays 7 pm to 10.30 pm). Telephone: 0992 572142.

How to get there: Between North Weald and Epping turn left on a minor road signposted to Coopersale. Drive through this village and downhill to a T-junction. Turn left past the Theydon Oak to Fiddlers Hamlet.

Parking: You may park at the pub but please let the licensee know before you set out on your walk.

Length of the walk: 3 miles. Map: OS Landranger 167 Chelmsford and Harlow (inn GR 473010).

This varied walk certainly combines the old and the new. Two crossings of the M11 are first under it, through a tunnel, and then over it, by means of a pedestrian bridge. These encounters at a safe distance from motorway traffic are separated by a delightful walk by way of Mount End and Beachet Wood, where a short unmade section of the Roman road from London to Great Dunmow is walked, and by grand views over the Roding valley.

The Walk
As you leave the pub turn left to the T-junction and turn right along Mount Road which after 350 yards passes under the M11. Please keep well into the side as the occasional car can be unforgiving. Through the tunnel you continue past Hornes Farm. Just beyond a road intersection on the left, turn left off the road at a footpath signpost and continue in your original direction with a hedge on your right to a stile. Cross this and another some yards further on. Pass to the left of Sawkins Farm and cross a stile to reach the road at Mount End. With its woods, hills and dales this is a very picturesque part of Essex. The

13

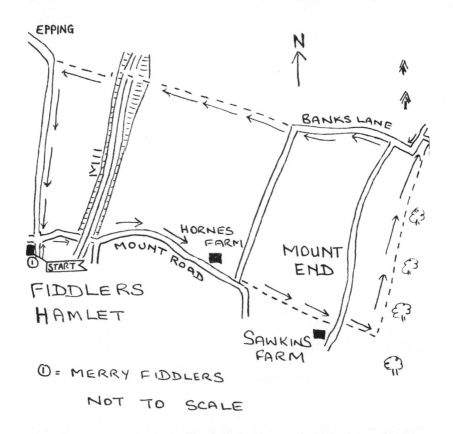

EPPING

N

BANKS LANE

HORNES FARM

MOUNT ROAD

MOUNT END

① START

FIDDLERS HAMLET

SAWKINS FARM

① = MERRY FIDDLERS

NOT TO SCALE

Roman road from Mount End to Hobbs Cross excited archaeologists when Roman remains were discovered there. Hereabouts grows the scarlet pimpernel. In sunny weather its flowers open at 8 am and close around 2 pm. Check your watches!

Turn left and immediately right over another stile to follow a fence on your right as far as Beachet Wood. Do not enter the wood but turn left and climb the path alongside all the way to a road. Turn left and left again to walk downhill along Banks Lane. The road dips down then climbs again to the corner where there is a public bridleway sign. Follow this track with views to the left over the Roding valley and the impressive-looking buildings of Gaynes Park to your right. Gaynes Park Hall is a fine large manor house which is in the parish of

14

Theydon Garnon. It dates mainly from the 18th century but contains some 16th and 17th century panelling, and has been in the possession of the Chisenhale Marsh family since 1780.

When you reach the end of the field turn right towards the bridge crossing the M11. The bridge is fenced in the middle to segregate private traffic from Gaynes Park and horses and pedestrians on the bridleway. Over the bridge the path is inside the field and crosses a short bridge. You pass the lodge and emerge from the next little field near the road. Turn left along this road and walk back to the Merry Fiddlers.

Nearby Coopersale House was the residence of the Archer Houblon family. The name Archer was awarded by Henry V in honour of the success of an English landowner ancestor at the Battle of Agincourt. In the 18th century, eccentric millionaire John Archer left the mansion and lived like a hermit in a tiny cottage. He continued to employ the servants and the gardeners but they were under strict instructions not to carry out their duties. Coopersale House was left undisturbed for a quarter of a century until Mr Archer's death. Some say he was taking revenge on the house, which he blamed for the death of his wife.

South Weald
3

The Tower Arms

Nearby Brentwood is fortunate in having two splendid country parks to the north and south of the town. The one to the north at South Weald was originally known as South Weald Park. It has since been renamed Weald Country Park and is a delight. In and around the park are some fascinating reminders of some of England's history. It was once owned by Waltham Abbey, but after the Dissolution, in the 16th century, Henry VIII sold it to Brian Tube, the Royal treasurer, who built Weald Hall north-west of the church next to the established deer park. Nearly 400 years later, during the Second World War, the park was requisitioned for military training. As a consequence the perimeter fence was broken and the deer escaped. The hall was then badly damaged by fire, and had to be demolished in 1950.

The Tower Arms takes its name from the Tower family, who bought the estate in 1752 and made many changes during the two centuries of their ownerhsip. Christopher Tower sold the park in 1946 to Metropolitan Railway Estates. A year later this company approached the county with an offer of the improved park at a price which was refused. All the magnificent contents of the Hall, including precious paintings, were auctioned, and after four years in a state of disrepair the building was finally demolished in 1950. When the park was sold, all the open areas became agricultural tenancies. In 1948 it was rumoured that the ploughing subsidy was to be lifted. The south-eastern part of the park was ploughed with 12 tractors, and so a hundred acres of ancient grassland with its wealth of plant and insect life was destroyed overnight – all for nothing, as no change was made to the subsidy. What does remain in the park today are scattered oaks and hornbeams, some as old as 500 years.

The inn was originally called the Spread Eagle and was at the west side of the church. In 1870 the Tower family bought the pub and renamed it the Tower Arms. It moved to its present site, right opposite the church – a fine setting in this charming hill-top village – in 1921. The church has Norman stones in its walls, and high above the churchyard are the rookeries of the park. Though sadly Weald Hall has gone there are several fine old buildings in and about the village. For many years a private family ran the Tower Arms. Now owned by Scottish and Newcastle Breweries, it is managed with some style and offers good, home-cooked food ranging from snacks to more substantial meals. There is an excellent selection of real ales – Greene King IPA, Young's SPA, Brakspear Bitter and Ruddles County – with Strongbow cider for the apple lovers. Meals are available in the evenings and from 12 noon to 2 pm. The Tower Arms is open from 11.30 am to 3 pm (12 noon to 3 pm Sundays) and 6 pm to 11 pm (7 pm to 10.30 pm Sundays). The Tower has long welcomed children, and it has a family room to the west side. The more recently constructed restaurant is also fine for the family. Outside is a lovely sloping garden and to this has been added a climbing frame and swing. Pétanque (French boules) is played here, and you are welcome to try your hand at this; just ask at the bar.

Telephone: 0277 210266

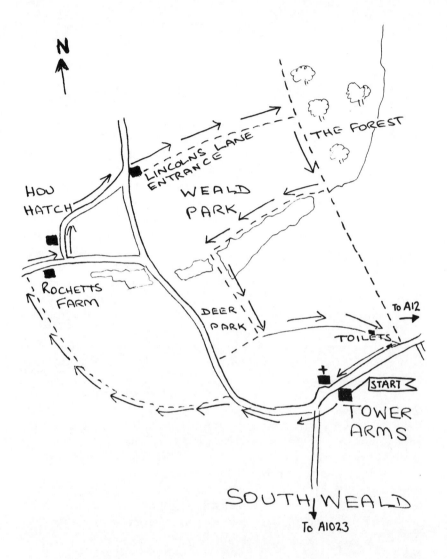

NOT TO SCALE

How to get there: Make for junction 28 on the M25 or by way of the A12. Take the exit to Brentwood. Past the Post House hotel turn left and cross above the A12. At the top of the hill turn right, and the Tower Arms is opposite the church.

18

Parking: You may park at the pub, but please ask the manager before setting out on your walk.

Length of the walk: 3½ miles. Map: OS Landranger 167 Chelmsford and Harlow (inn GR 572938).

A pleasant walk which takes you through the Weald Country Park. There is a hillside picnic area where the hunger pangs of children (and adults) can be satisfied while admiring the views across the surrounding countryside. The return journey takes you past the lake and deer enclosure.

The Walk

Turn left outside the pub and make your way with care on the grass verge down and round following the road. You will reach a concrete footpath sign opposite the main entrance to the park. Follow this to the left, crossing a stile. The path is waymarked and goes west and north-west through a thicket to follow an iron fence. When the fence ends, continue in the same direction across a field – the path is usually marked. You come to a crossing hedge and go through this by a bridge and stile.

South Weald Church.

19

Continue onwards over the next field and reach a road by way of another stile. Turn right (east) and when the road sweeps right turn left up a wide track.

Soon you reach Lincoln's Lane and follow a public footpath sign into the park. Up the hill there are picnic tables and certainly from here is a fine view over Brentwood. Continue on (east) into the wood and turn right (south). When you reach the lake turn right (west) along the north side turning left at the end. Follow the path by the deer enclosure then bear left and climb over open ground going south-eastwards to reach the public toilets. Through the car park there is a footpath sign pointing into the park. Exit the park here and turn right along an elevated footpath to reach the church and the Tower Arms.

In Wigley Bush Lane, near the school, is Luptons, where Robert Ind (of Ind Coope, the brewers) lived in 1848. His business partner, Octavius Coope MP, resided at Rochetts, opposite Weald Park. Across the road from Luptons is Wealdcote, a 16th century building.

4 **Ashdon**
The Rose and Crown

Ashdon is a very attractive village in the north of the county, barely 2 miles from the Cambridgeshire border going north and less than 1 mile going east. The country hereabouts is hilly and well wooded, mainly with oak and ash, and it is ideal for short walks. Within the Ashdon parish are the Bartlow hills – a group of burial mounds of Romano-British origin, the biggest being 40 ft high and 150 ft across.

The village pub is often amongst the oldest buildings in the district, and the Rose and Crown is no exception. One timbered room has a pool table, darts and other games, while another timbered room is particularly good for children. The Cromwell lounge has wall paintings dating back to 1643 – some behind glass are unrestored. These were painted by monks from the priory at Ashdon.

In the bar there is a wide choice of food and drink. The food is mostly home made, with chicken masala a particularly good speciality. Real ales are Greene King IPA and Tolly Cobbold

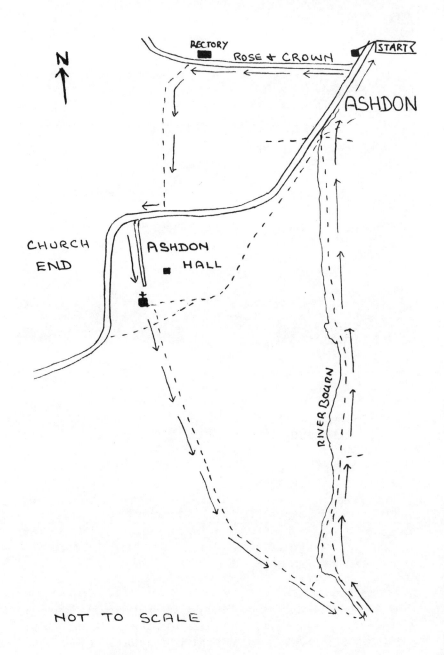

N

RECTORY

ROSE + CROWN

START

ASHDON

CHURCH
END

ASHDON
HALL

RIVER BOURN

NOT TO SCALE

Original. The cider is Taunton Dry Blackthorn. Opening hours are 11.30 am to 2.30 pm (12 noon to 3 pm Sundays) and 6 pm to 11 pm (7 pm to 10.30 pm Sundays). Food is not served on Wednesdays. At the rear of the car park is a very large garden with swings and things, or you can just sit and enjoy the village environs.
Telephone: 0799 584337.

How to get there: Approach Ashdon by driving north through Thaxted. Turn right on the B1051 to Great Sampford and straight on at the crossroads near Radwinter. Three miles further north you reach the centre of Ashdon.

Parking: There is a large car park off the road behind the pub. You are welcome to park there but please let the landlord know before leaving for your walk.

Length of the walk: 2½ miles. Map: OS Landranger 154 Cambridge and Newmarket (inn GR 588422).

The walk is in two halves. The firt half ascends to the Old Rectory, goes through the churchyard and proceeds at height with fine views before descending to Water End. The second half follows the river Bourn in the valley past some picturesque old cottages back to the village.

The Walk
From the front door of the Rose and Crown turn right for a few yards then right again up Rectory Lane. The age of this lane is evidenced by the extent to which it has sunk below the fields on either side. When you come to a large red-brick building on the right (the 400-year-old rectory) turn left along a track some height above the village, which is now nowhere to be seen. As you walk along this contour, ignore the crossing yellow arrows, and just before reaching the road, turn right along a footway which leads you opposite the church by the building of the Ashdon National School. This was founded in 1841 by the rector and was part of a movement at the time to provide education with a strong religious bias. The money was put up by the rector and some other wealthy members of the parish, and for a while Ashdon maintained two schools. However, not

23

The village hall, Ashdon.

many years later the rector applied for the school to be 'taken into union' with the board school and it was closed in 1855, later to be used as a sunday school.

Cross the road and walk towards the church, which is nearly 700 years old. In the church a lovely chancel roof was set up about the time of the Battle of Agincourt (1415). Both porches are fifteenth century and so are a chest and a moulded roofbeam. Stone carvings of a knight and a woman each behind a shield are at the windows in the chapel, which has a timber roof. There are many pieces of glass about 500 years old including an angel with golden wings. To the east of the church is a meadow which is believed to be the site of a deserted village dating from before the 13th century.

To the left of the church cross a stile, turn right and walk over the field to another stile. Observe the Guildhall on your right, which is 500 years old. The first recorded mention of the Guildhall was in 1518. It had been built for meetings of the guild and later it became accommodation for the poor. In 1775 it was converted into a workhouse, then, in 1839, it became three dwellings. The building was restored in 1955.

Cross the stile and follow a track which climbs between two fields. As you climb look back at the church to admire the different aspect from that distance. Eventually you pass through a hedge gap and turn left downhill. First there are two stiles to be crossed into and out of a narrow field and another stile brings you to Water End. You may wish to walk on a few yards to see the delightful setting of this streamside hamlet. Turn left up a track at a bridleway sign and walk near but above the side of the river Bourn. This is a contrast – the walk, previously along ridges, is now in a valley. Just past a stile on your left walk through the garden of a cottage – there is a nifty Wendy house here, and a yellow arrow guides you between the cottage and the outbuildings. Soon you reach more cottages (Hill Farm is above you). Finally you come to a series of three bridleway bridges which bring you to a track leading to the road. Turn right along this with care for 350 yards back to the Rose and Crown.

Blackmore
The Bull

The glory of Blackmore is the church tower. It is built in three stages – pagoda-like – in diminishing scale, capped by a tall spire. Seen from the fields at all points of the compass around the village it is a lovely sight. Some parts of the church are Norman but the tower was built in the 15th century. Near the church is a house called Jericho, frequently visited by Henry VIII; indeed his bastard son, Henry Fitzroy, was born here. When Henry would suddenly ride away from his court his courtiers would wink and say 'He's gone to Jericho'.

In Church Street there are several old houses in good repair including the Bull itself. This excellent pub predates the church tower and probably provided lodging for Henry's men when he visited Jericho. The Bull has a ghost in residence, but fear not: it is only ever heard in the middle of the night when it will call out your name either in a male or a female voice. If you doubt this story speak to some of the staff who have occasionally stayed overnight, but do not wish to do so again.

The real ales usually available are Tetley, Tolly Cobbold and Burton Ale, and Taunton Dry Blackthorn cider is on tap. Opening hours are from 11 am to 3 pm (12 noon to 3 pm Sundays) and 6 pm to 11 pm (7 pm to 10.30 pm Sundays). A wide range of home-made food, from sandwiches to steaks, is available, which will satisfy most tastes. There is a large garden at the back with children's games. During the day the public bar is converted into a family lunch-room and children with their parents are welcome.

Telephone: 0277 821208.

How to get there: Blackmore is signposted off the A414 Ongar to Chelmsford road. It is also signposted from the A128 north of Brentwood.

Parking: Park at the pub with the usual proviso of requesting permission from the landlord before setting out on your walk.

Length of the walk: 2¼ miles. Map: OS Landranger 167 Chelmsford and Harlow (inn GR 604018).

This walk is a pleasing mix of country lanes, farmland and paths. On the way you pass Blackmore's church with its impressive tower, cross the river Wid and return to a classic village pond at Blackmore Green. Watch out also for the village stocks.

The Walk
From the pub turn left down Church Street. It is like walking through history as the street has the feel of the days 400 years ago when Henry VIII's servants made their way from the Bull to the house of Jericho to serve the King. A priory was founded here in 1152, but a few stones in the garden of Jericho and parts of the church are all that is left of it. The building was pulled down at Henry VIII's command. In the church the massive beams show the way craftsmen built things to last. The font is more than 500 years old.

At the church entrance turn right to a concrete footpath sign pointing through the churchyard to a stile just by the tower and close to a high red-brick wall. Cross the stile and continue with the wall on your left to cross a bridge over the moat. A path

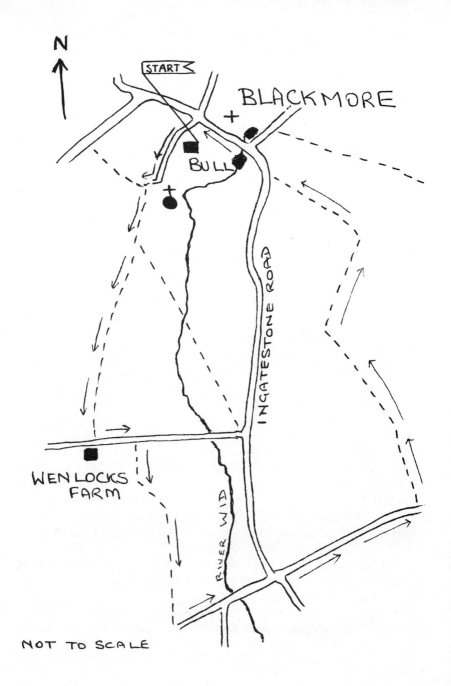

N

START

BLACKMORE

BULL

INGATESTONE ROAD

WENLOCKS
FARM

RIVER WID

NOT TO SCALE

The church lych gate, Blackmore.

across the field is usually visible leading to Wenlocks Farm which you reach through a gap in the hedge at a concrete footpath sign. Turn left down Wenlocks Lane for 130 yards and turn right at a wooden footpath sign and cross a stile. Walk across the field, keeping the pond on your right, and turn right over a stile/bridge/stile combination. After crossing this, turn left and walk beside a hedge to reach a stile in the corner. A short, sometimes muddy path by a stream leads you to a bridge and stile. Walk on and when you shortly come to a mature hedge keep it on your left coming to another stile and bridge. Here a yellow marker on a post directs you on but at this point the route turns left down a rough farm track to a metal gate. This should be open but if it is locked you can pass round the left post. You have now reached Hay Green Lane and shortly come to Clatterford Wash where the river Wid crosses the lane. For times of flood there is an elevated footway to assist the pedestrian.

Now you pass some very large houses and come to a crossroads. Follow the road signposted to Ingatestone for 500 yards and turn left at a concrete footpath sign. Walk across the field diagonally to a stile to the left of a metal gate. The next field is narrow and you walk towards the far right-hand corner (north/west). At the corner turn right through a ditch (no bridge at present) and follow the field edge with a hedge on your left. At a broad gap change sides and continue till you reach the remains of a hedge to your left. Now turn left across the field aiming for the petrol station 300 yards away. At the road there is a gap in the hedge and a concrete footpath sign. Turn right and then left over the Wid which at this point is widened into two large ponds. Walk over the green and enter the back garden of the Bull through a gap in the fence. You will have passed the village stocks which may be useful should any member of your party have been especially trying!

Another medieval phenomenon, the Black Death, reached Essex, from the Continent, in 1349. The records are scant but the rolls of the manor of Fingrith in Blackmore provide a valuable insight into this catastrophe. By June 1349 55 of its tenants had died. In all, 70 tenants plus unrecorded wives, children and domestic servants were lost. Sound evidence exists that half the population of the village perished. A legacy from that time is the so-called 'plague route' round the north of the village, avoiding the centre. Blackmore was on the main track from Chelmsford to London and travellers made a road which now passes Redrose Farm and continues by the village hall on a byway to regain the main road at the west end.

6 Great Dunmow
The Chequers

Dunmow is a pleasant little town. It goes about it business purposefully enough, and though scarcely a tourist attraction it has appealing features some of which you will encounter on the route of this walk. The town is perhaps best known for the Dunmow flitch (of bacon), which is awarded to the couple who have not quarrelled within a year and a day of celebrating their marriage, and is said to date back to the 13th century. The priory, from which the custom sprang, was a home of Augustinian canons, set up by Lady Juga Baynard whose husband had fought at Hastings; indeed, Chaucer's Wife of Bath made the comment 'The bacoun . . . that some men han in Essex at Dunmowe'. By the reign of Henry VIII the priory was in decline and closed in 1536. The buildings were destroyed except for a small part of the church.

Right in the town centre, round the corner from the Saracen's Head Hotel, stands the Chequers, a traditional oak-beamed pub, but with a children's room to make families feel at home. It was

31

owned by Allied Breweries but is now a freehouse. The real ales served are Greene King IPA plus an occasional guest beer, and Strongbow cider is on draught. Snacks and more substantial meals are available – ploughman's, sandwiches, huffers and cooked offerings, eggs, sausages, steaks etc. Within the children's room is a pool table, and cards or cribbage can also be played. In the garden such pursuits as pétanque and a bouncing bus can be enjoyed. If you are delayed with all these activities bed and breakfast can be arranged. The Chequers is open all day from 11 am to 11 pm (12 noon to 3 pm and 7 pm to 10.30 pm Sundays).

Telephone: 0371 872546.

How to get there: Make for Great Dunmow centre. At the point where three roads meet by the Saracen's Head Hotel, go west along Stortford Road for 50 yards and the Chequers is on the corner of Chequers Lane.

Parking: Park in the pub car park but please ask for permission to leave the car while you do the walk.

Length of the walk: 2 miles. Map: OS Landranger 167 Chelmsford and Harlow (inn GR 627220).

Dunmow means 'meadows on the hill', and it is through these by the river Chelmer that you walk to reach the parish church with a 14th century tower and fine old buildings around it. There follows a short climb up Beaumont Hill with views over the river valley. The return journey passes the delightful Doctor's Pond.

The Walk
From the pub turn right and walk down the road to the Saracen's Head Hotel. Cross the High Street and turn right into White Street, soon turning left down Mill Lane. Pass the Catholic church, St Mary the Virgin, and turn left along a track between the last house and a fence. This track crosses a road and goes out to a meadow, not far from the river Chelmer. The path turns left going north, and when it reaches a football field goes left again through a gap in the hedge. Turn right and follow with the hedge on your right. At the end of the field turn right

32

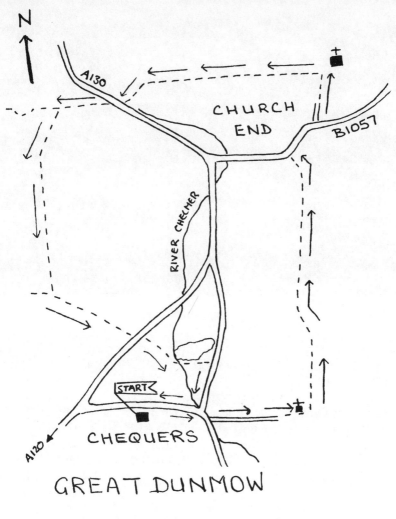

N

A130

CHURCH
END

B1057

RIVER CHELMER

START

CHEQUERS

A120

GREAT DUNMOW

NOT TO SCALE

through a gap in the hedge then bear left out to the corner of a road by the Angel and Harp public house and the parish church.

Before entering the church, look for the monkey and the lion carved on the tower above the window, an array of monsters

Near Dunmow church; 15th century Clock House with shaped gables.

as waterspouts, a 700-year-old coffin lid, and a set of Roman tiles. The church is rich in possessions, having a 14th century font, a brass portrait of Elizabethan Philippa Glascock, and a carved oak tablet on the wall, remembering one of our boys who fell at Gaza, 'marching to the promised land'. The church hero, however, is the vicar Edward Noel Mellish who won the VC in the First World War – the first chaplain to win it.

Walk through the churchyard and just past the Old Vicarage turn left on a green path between fields, walking uphill on Beaumont Hill. Turn and look back for some splendid views of the hill above the river Chelmer.

The path leads to a road which you cross and turn right up a narrow side lane. When you reach a gap turn left passing over two stiles to an open field. Follow the well-marked path to a gap in a wall. At a hedge turn left and immediately right to walk south-east with fences on the left past a pond to a farm. Keep straight on downhill over a road and past the Doctor's Pond out to the road near Luckin's wine store. Turn right up to the Saracen's Head Hotel and so back to the Chequers.

7 **Herongate**
The Old Dog Inn

Herongate has always been an attractive village but for many years it was marred by the dense traffic travelling on the A128, a road number which struck fear into the inhabitants of the Brentwood area. When the M25 was opened the improvement was immediate, and though it is still rather more than a quiet road this village has greatly benefited.

About ¾ mile off the A128 along the Billericay road at a sharp bend to the left lies the Old Dog Inn. A fine old weatherboarded building, it has been a freehouse for many years. It is said that one in five country pubs in Essex is haunted, and this may be one of them. A large car park is positioned close to the pub but tucked away behind hedges. The present licensees provide food and drink of the best quality. Inside, the bar is wide and unusually shallow but a good-sized back room welcomes families with their drinks, and also doubles as a restaurant. A large selection of food is on offer from snacks to main meals, and dishes available include lasagne, beef and venison pie,

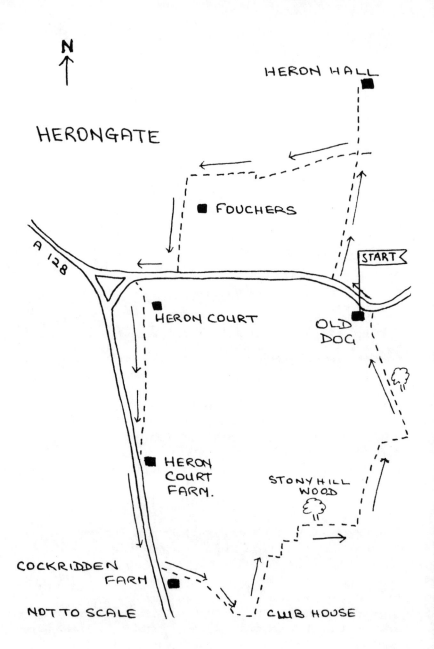

N

HERONGATE

HERON HALL

FOUCHERS

A 128

START

HERON COURT

OLD DOG

HERON COURT FARM.

STONY HILL WOOD

COCKRIDDEN FARM

NOT TO SCALE

CLUB HOUSE

always a vegetarian dish, garlic salmon and steaks. A children's menu offers half portions of everything on the main menu plus things like 'shanty' fish fingers and egg dishes. The real ale range is impressive, sometimes there are as many as 20 on offer – Adnams, Greene King IPA and Abbot Ale, Nethergate, the Mauldons range, and all the Crouch Vales, plus rarer brews from all over England.

Opening hours are from 10.30 am to 2.30 pm and 6 pm to 11 pm Monday to Saturday (12 noon to 3 pm and 7 pm to 10.30 pm Sundays).

Telephone: 0277 810337.

How to get there: At the southern end of Herongate village turn off the A128 taking the road signposted to Billericay. The Old Dog Inn is on the right, ¾ mile along this road.

Parking: Park at the pub but please ask at the bar before leaving your car to go on the walk.

Length of the walk: 2¾ miles. Map: OS Landranger 177 East London (inn GR 641910).

This walk will take just over one hour. It passes Heron Hall, once the home of a distinguished family, the Tyrells. North-west of the Hall, if you wish to stray off the route, it is possible to view a heronry, for herons were indeed once bred here. The walking route goes west through the village, then southwards close to the A128 to Cockridden Farm. The final stretch crosses a golf course to Dog Wood with impressive views over the Thames basin.

The Walk

Turn left from the pub and walk along the roadside on a green verge. Cross the road to the pavement past some houses. Turn right at a signpost announcing bridleway 47 to Lapwater Hall. Don't be deterred by a private road notice – this relates to motor traffic, not walkers. As you near Heron Hall, turn left along footpath 46 with the hedge on your left, crossing two bridges to turn left by a ditch to Fouchers Farm. A yellow waymark directs you to the left through the farm buildings to Billericay Road by a concrete footpath sign. Turn right for a few yards to the Boars Head tavern. Just past the pub turn left along

Fouchers Farm entrance, Herongate.

Heron Chase walking between the Boars Head and a large duck-pond. The path passes Heron Court, a large attractive house and soon reaches Button Farm. Take the path forking left to cross a stile and follow the waymarks past the buildings through a field to a stile by a footpath sign close to the A128.

There is a wide verge to walk on by the busy road and you will soon come to what was Cockridden Farm, now Stonyhill Golf Club, but provision has been made for the rights of way to be maintained. Follow the track heading towards the club house turning left behind a pond at a waymark. Cross the hedge and turn left towards Stonyhill Wood. The path goes round the southern edge of the wood which in spring is bathed in bluebells. At the end of the wood turn left to a hedge line. The path is on the north side of the hedge running east. At a gap in the hedge after about 250 yards an arrow points to the left and you make your way north-east to a corner in the hedge ahead where two plank bridges cross a ditch. Continue east along the hedge to Dog Wood. Now turn left to a stile and then a gate leading to the back of the Old Dog Inn.

Finchingfield
The Finch Inn

Finchingfield is often the object of tourists who come to explore the picturesque village. Once visited it is not easily forgotten. A brook flows through the village into the river Pant. In the centre of the village it widens into a large pond. Here, houses keep their distance, probably because the brook tends to flood. Hardly a house or cottage lacks charm. The farms are 400 years old, and the windmill, the Guildhall and the church are all set gloriously into the composition. The grand old church dominates the scene and all these provide a heritage of rural beauty that few villages can excel.

Finchingfield was a clearing or open space in the forest in which primitive cultivation was carried on by the people of 'Finc', as it was known. The Conquest in 1066 left a lasting influence on the countryside, giving us farm and manor names still used today. Spains Hall was named after Ralph de Ispania; Cornish Hall from Richard de Cornett; and Boyton Hall after Julian de Boyton.

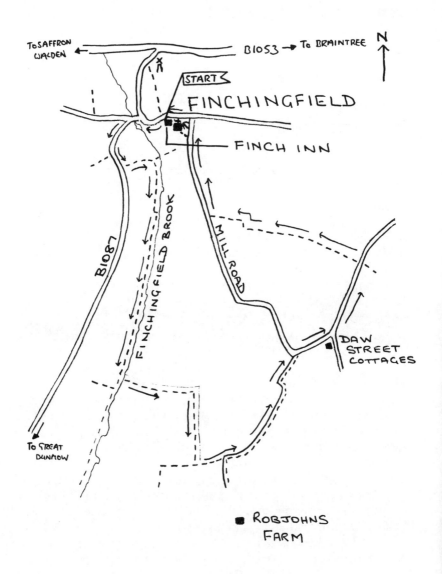

To SAFFRON WALDEN

B1053 → To BRAINTREE

N

START

FINCHINGFIELD

FINCH INN

B1087

FINCHINGFIELD BROOK

MILL ROAD

DAW STREET COTTAGES

To GREAT DUNMOW

■ ROBJOHNS FARM

NOT TO SCALE

Formerly an Ind Coope pub called the Green Man, the Finch Inn is now a freehouse. The policy on beer is always to have Greene King IPA and Courage Directors with up to four varying guest beers. Also Strongbow cider is on tap. One of the rooms is now a restaurant and it is here that under-14s can be welcomed with their adult companions. There is a good selection of food available. Home-cooked ham and pies are particularly to be recommended and there are also huffers with assorted fillings. At the rear is a large car park and a spacious garden with ladders and swings. Given reasonable weather you may prefer to partake of solid and liquid sustenance in the open air. The Finch is open from 11 am to 3 pm, 6.30 pm to 11 pm Mondays to Saturdays, and 12 noon to 3 pm, 7 pm to 10.30 pm on Sundays.

Telephone: 0371 810407.

How to get there: Travel on the B1057 from Great Dunmow through Great Bardfield. Cross the river in the centre of Finchingfield and bear right towards the church. Just before you get there the Finch Inn is on the right.

Parking: Park at the pub but please ask the licensee for permission to leave your car while taking a short walk.

Length of the walk: 2¼ miles. Map: OS Landranger 168 Chelmsford and Harlow (inn GR 686328).

The walk passes through the centre of the village by the duck-pond before joining a path going south close to the banks of the Finchingfield brook for just over ½ mile. After crossing a wooden bridge we climb to a height from where there are fine views of Wethersfield to the east and Great Bardfield to the south. As Robjohns Farm and the large lake come into sight the route turns north and west to join Mill Road into Finchingfield, with several fine old buildings to be seen. Finally we walk through the churchyard and under the arch of the Guildhall out to the street close to the Finch Inn.

The Walk

Turn left outside the pub and walk between the pond and houses on your left. Keep on the pavement for several yards until a footpath sign points left. Follow this path towards the

The Finch Inn is the building next to the church at the top of the street.

Finchingfield brook. Before reaching the bridge turn right along a fenced track and follow this path for about ½ mile, sometimes close to the brook. Ignore the first concrete bridge, but after crossing the lawn behind the long garden of a house on the road above, turn left over a wooden slatted bridge. I counted 22 slats.

Now climb up the green path with a hedge to your left. At the field corner turn right and continue on until you reach a gravelly road leading down to Robjohns Farm and a large lake. Turn left and walk on the concrete track to a road. Take the right turn for 100 yards to Daw Street Cottages. Turn left signposted to Wethersfield. When you reach two footpath signposts follow the concrete one on the left on a good path through the middle of the field. On the way cross a little bridge with a rail before coming to Mill Road. Turn right and pass some old houses, including the Old Priory and the school, to reach the churchyard. Now walk past the church and under the Guildhall Arch to the street a few steps from the Finch Inn. The Guildhall, a timber and plaster building with old casement windows and chimneys, has a fine kingpost truss in its roof.

42

The church, which stands on the site of a previous model, dates from 1170 and is an excellent example of Norman influence and art. The tower was extended during the 15th century and surmounted by a tall spire. This spire was blown down in 1658 and some years later replaced by the present 18th century lantern. Two screens in the church are of considerable interest, and the chancel dates from the 15th century.

Looking up the hill towards the church, you can see an imposing four-shaft chimney stack. This is part of a 17th century house which was the parish workhouse. As the records show, 'Sunday and Wednesday in every week the poor to have a hot dinner of pudding, meat, and vegetables, roots or such like and a reasonable sufficiency. At other times bread and cheese for dinner and supper, also gruel, broth or milk for breakfast made hot, also of good wholesome small beer at dinner and supper. The poor who will pay for drink are allowed to have it in the house, but the Master will not allow them so much as to get intoxicated.'

9 Galleywood Common
The Horse and Groom

On the high ground, to the south of Chelmsford, Galleywood Common has several strings to its bow. The wild parts are a mass of gorse, shining gold when in full bloom. The church spire rises to 127 ft. For many years there was a racecourse, parts of which still remain, encircling both the common and the church as well as crossing the road. The necessary road closure on race days was no doubt one of the reasons why racing was discontinued in the 1930s. For our purposes there is a fine old pub right on the common.

The central part of the Horse and Groom is 500 years old, with no doubt many a tale to be told of the racing days. It is owned by Grays, formerly a Chelmsford brewer, now a beer wholesaler but still with tenanted houses throughout Essex. This one appears to be sited in just the right place. Real ales available are Ridleys Mild and Greene King IPA and Abbot Ale, while Dry Blackthorn cider is on draught. An excellent variety of food is available every lunchtime except Sunday – Japanese-

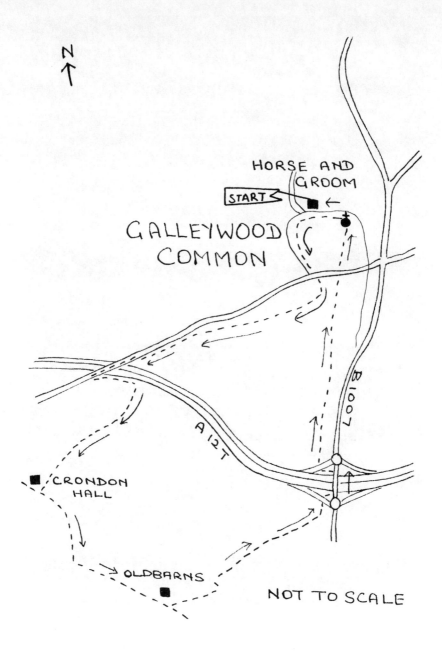

N

HORSE AND GROOM

START

GALLEYWOOD COMMON

B1007

A12T

CRONDON HALL

OLDBARNS

NOT TO SCALE

St Michael and All Angels, Galleywood.

style prawns took my fancy but most tastes will be satisfied by various soups, seven assorted salads, sandwiches, ploughman's, tandoori chicken wings, grilled gammon, breaded scampi or plaice, chicken curry, lasagne and burgers. Eating in the evening is possible Thursday to Saturday but an advance call can enable service on other evenings and Sunday lunchtime as well. For the family there is a pleasant little room with seating, some tables and games. This room is at the bottom end of the building. Those who are 14-plus can enjoy a game of pool with their parents in the public bar. The saloon bar has several tables and a longer bar. Outdoors there are several picnic tables looking on to the common.

Opening hours are from 11 am to 3 pm, 6 pm to 11 pm Monday to Saturday, 12 noon to 3 pm and 7 pm to 10.30 pm on Sunday.

Telephone: 0245 261653.

How to get there: The B1007 connects Chelmsford with Stock. Just north of the Running Mare pub on the same side of the road turn into Goat Hall Lane. Take the next turning on the left which is Horse and Groom Lane. The pub is off the end of the lane.

Parking: At the pub on the common. Please let the landlord know before setting out on the walk.

Length of the walk: 3¾ miles. Map: OS Landranger 167 Chelmsford and Harlow (inn GR 701029).

The walk, though affected by the Chelmsford bypass built in the 80s, is nevertheless a good one, contriving two elevated crossings of the busy road and some fine views of the Wid valley.

The Walk

Walk from the pub behind the white railings on to part of the old racetrack. Flat racing was first held at Galleywood in 1759, and in 1800 a steeplechase course was laid out and a new stand built. Our walk passes the site of the grandstand. There are few, if any, racetracks which go round a church as Galleywood did.

Turn right and follow the course to a road. Cross the road to the right of some green wooden buildings following a yellow arrow waymark. At the end of the wood on your right turn right down a path through the wood. On reaching a field turn right following the edge of a field and then out to a road. This leads over a bridge. Turn left by a bridleway sign and follow this muddy track for 150 yards, turning right into a green lane. You walk downhill over a stream and up to a farm road by Crondon Hall which lies on a splendid slope in the Wid valley, but as in many parts of Essex the word 'Hall' describes a farmhouse. Turn left through the farm buildings and on to Oldbarns. Turn left at a footpath sign on a field path. Pass through one wooded section and along the right side of Lady Grove, with views on the left of the Wid valley and beyond. Cross two stiles on to the side of the embankment at the bypass turning right over rough ground to reach the slip road. Cross the bridge to your left and make your way to the common. Now walk on to the north. Cross a farm access road before reaching the road with white railings. Bear right and walk to the church (the spire should be apparent).

St Michael and All Angels church bears itself with the assured air of a Victorian middle-class suburban church – all yellow brick with red dressings. The spire is a familiar landmark for miles around like its fellow at nearby Widford. It was built in the mid 19th century, many years after racing at Galleywood first started. It must have been an odd sight if the builders laid down their tools to join the form followers on high days and holidays.

Now follow the racetrack left to return to the Horse and Groom.

10 Castle Hedingham
The Bell Inn

To walk in the vicinity of Hedingham Castle from the village of
Castle Hedingham is to share in a stateliness unequalled in Essex
and possibly unsurpassed in England. For 600 years the castle
was held by the de Veres and the keep is the finest of its period
still in existence.

Castle Hedingham was also the chief hop-growing centre in
Essex as early as the 16th century. The hop was a precarious
crop, yielding nothing in some years but handsome proceeds in
others. By 1887, after 300 years of continuous cultivation, hop-
growing had died out in the area. As a by-product, hop poles
were no longer needed and many Essex woodlands lost much
of their value.

The Bell is a 500-year-old coaching inn with unique historical
connections. Disraeli held political meetings here before dining
at the castle. There are separate bars, the public and the saloon,
as well as two sitting-rooms which can accommodate children
accompanied by adults. There is a good variety of excellent bar

food including smoked prawns with a garlic dip, pot meals such as haddock and prawn gratinée, steak and Guinness pie, and spicy Turkish chicken. Real ales are Greene King IPA and Abbot Ale served by gravity straight from the barrel. There is also a local cider – Castlings Heath Cottage. You can take your dog in but please give advance warning as the licensee has a Great Dane who is not keen on other dogs in the pub but can be confined during your visit. When the weather is right use may be made of the large garden at the rear.

Not so old as the pub is the rear wing which has an unusual barrel ceiling. This was built as a theatre and also used as a court house. The Bell is still a centre for entertainment in the village, with a jazz band on the last Sunday lunchtime of each month, and songs to a guitar every Friday evening. I think you will want to return again to this superb pub and explore more walks in the district. Opening hours are from 11.30 am to 3 pm and 6 pm to 11 pm Monday to Saturday, 12 noon to 3 pm and 7 pm to 10.30 pm on Sunday.

Telephone: 0787 460350.

How to get there: Drive north from Colchester on the A604 or from Braintree on the A131 to join the A604. Through Sible Hedingham turn right on a road signposted to Castle Hedingham which you reach after ¾ mile.

Parking: Street parking is available but you may park at the Bell. Please let it be known that you are parked in the pub car park before setting off on your walk.

Length of the walk: 2 miles. Map: OS Landranger 155 Bury St Edmunds and Sudbury area (inn GR 786355).

This gentle stroll through woods and past farmland affords some excellent views of Hedingham Castle along the way.

The Walk
Leaving the Bell turn right to follow the road for 300 yards. Nearly opposite the New Park a concrete footpath post on the pavement opposite points uphill along a track through woods. When the woods end the path continues with the hedge on the

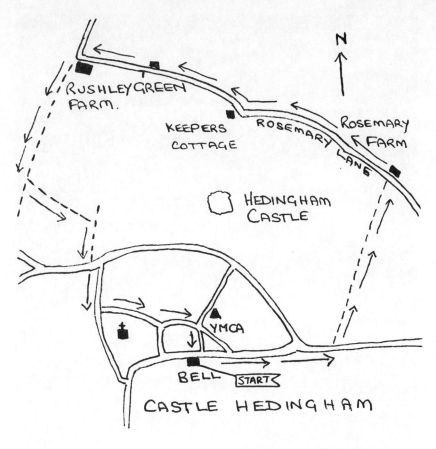

N

RUSHLEY GREEN FARM.

KEEPERS COTTAGE

ROSEMARY LANE

ROSEMARY FARM

HEDINGHAM CASTLE

YMCA

BELL

START

CASTLE HEDINGHAM

NOT TO SCALE

right to Rosemary Farm. Turn left along Rosemary Lane. Keep left to Keeper's Cottage, turning right to Rushley Green Farm. (Ignore two concrete footpath posts on the way.) Just past the farm take care to find a waymark post at the left-hand corner of the next house. Behind the post cross the stile and go through the metal gate and past a paddock fence. Turn left to reach a stile under an oak tree in the hedge corner opposite.

Cross the stile and follow with a hedge on your left passing Church Field Grove. When you reach another stile cross and turn left to take a good path downhill with fine views of the castle keep. Hedingham Castle is one of the great medieval

fortresses of Essex. The de Vere family held Hedingham for 600 years, and during the violent years of the Middle Ages the castle stood siege only twice, both times during the reign of King John. Robert de Vere was on the barons' side against the monarch and the castle was taken by the king, who left a garrison there to defend it against French invaders. In 1216, the Dauphin successfully besieged the castle. When Henry VII visited Hedingham Castle in 1498, John de Vere put on such a magnificent show that the king invoked a new law to check baronial power and fined his host £10,000 for his trouble!

At a T-junction of paths turn right to reach the village road. Turn left and immediately right along Crown Street by a house called Crosskeys. Turn left along Church Ponds with a fine view of the church. This is Norman in origin, although the red-brick tower is 17th century. Even more impressive than the chancel with its beautiful pointed windows, the great wheel window, and, above, the finest double hammer-beam roof in Essex, are the three Norman doorways with three Norman doors. One is fixed in place, while the other two swing, letting centuries of worshippers in and out. In the churchyard the shape and base of a 12th century cross have been set up in memory of the sons of Castle Hedingham who did not come back from the First World War. It was found in the cellar of the Falcon, a medieval inn which used to be in Falcon Square.

Past the church you come to Falcon Square. Bear left to the youth hostel, and right up Lucas Lane to the Bell Inn.

Just to the north of Castle Hedingham the Colne Valley steam trains frequently make their way along a line bought from British Rail. For those who can remember the age of steam, this will prove a nostalgic trip. For those who cannot, try the past for size!

11 Runsell Green, Danbury
The Anchor

Though often quoted as the highest point in Essex, Danbury is not quite that, but it is the highest village in Essex. The church stands at the top of the hill encircled by lovely woods and is well worth a visit. A short walk from the rear of the church offers a magnificent view of the southern landscape. Opposite the church is the Griffin Inn mentioned in Sir Walter Scott's novel *Waverley*. Indeed, the author is said to have written part of *Quenhoo Hall* while residing there. Much of the land is owned by the National Trust so protecting the village from most unwanted building developments.

A legend in Danbury recalls how the devil, in the midst of a tremendous storm, stole the fifth bell from the church belfry and carried it high in the air. Overcome from the weight he dropped it in a nearby wood on a hillside now known as Bell Hill Wood. A crater some 25 ft across and several ft deep exists to this day to show where the bell is said to have landed and still be hidden.

Another story concerns the embalmed knight of Danbury. In 1779 a Mrs Frances Ffytche died and a grave was dug for her; at about 30 inches below the pavement the workmen laid bare a huge flat stone under which was a lead coffin. It was decided to open the coffin in the expectation of seeing the bones of one of the knights whose effigy was laid on the tomb. Inside the lead coffin was found an elm coffin, and inside this a cement-covered shell ¾ inch thick. When the lid was removed, a young man with firm white flesh and perfect teeth was revealed. The preservation of his body was due to embalming liquid which half filled the coffin. After inspection by the villagers the coffin was lowered into the grave. Those who had seen the opened coffin had viewed the figure of a 500-year-old knight.

Runsell Green is a pretty little hamlet on the eastern outskirts of the village, with houses clustered round a triangular green. This hamlet formed the nucleus of a separate manor called Runsell, which was given to Canterbury Cathedral before the battle of Maldon in 991. A brick house on the left of the green was originally the Anchor but about 1830 it lost its sign to the house across the road. By the end of the 1830s the original Anchor was called the Saracen's Head, but finally closed in 1908. It continued as a bakery and grocery shop well into the present century. Meanwhile the 'new' Anchor was brewing and retailing beer. Gill House, another building on the green, was a pork butchers.

The Anchor belonged for many years to Bass Charrington, but fairly recently was purchased by Ridleys, a major Essex brewer. Real ales are Ridleys IPA, Adnams Bitter and Adnams Extra, with Strongbow cider on tap. A section of the bar to the right of the saloon and the adjoining conservatory are fine for children, and outdoors there are two gardens, one of which has swings and slides. Back inside, tempting dishes are advertised on blackboards. They range from ploughman's and French sticks with delicious fillings, to such choices as rack of lamb Anglaise or salmon tagliatelle, both strong favourites with the regular customers. The pub is open on Monday to Saturday from 11 am to 2.30 pm and 6 pm to 11 pm between October and April (all day from May till September) and on Sunday from 12 noon to 3 pm and 7 pm till 10.30 pm.

Telephone: 0245 222457.

How to get there: Danbury is bisected by the A414 bearing traffic from Chelmsford to Maldon. Runsell Green is at the eastern end of Danbury. A road (signposted to Woodham Walter) leaves the A414, and the Anchor is a few yards from that intersection.

Parking: Park at the pub but please ask the manager before setting out on your walk.

Length of the walk: 2¼ miles. Map: OS Landranger 168 Colchester and the Blackwater, and 167 Chelmsford and Harlow (inn GR 796054).

The Anchor Inn pub sign.

Walks in this area often take in some lovely woodland and this route is no exception, passing as it does through delightful Thrift Wood. The walk also follows the edge of a golf course, goes through some splendid fruit orchards and offers fine views over the Blackwater.

The Walk

Turn left from the Anchor and walk up the side of the green to the A414. Turn left for just over ½ mile. This is often a busy road but with a reasonable pavement all the way. Just after passing the Royal Oak at a concrete footpath signpost turn left and soon cross a stile to walk on a path towards the woods facing. These are called Thrift Wood and not many years ago hid a wild boar which had escaped from a transporting vehicle. Over many weeks, attempts were made to recapture the animal, without success. Eventually the pack from a passing hunt disturbed the boar and he ran out into the road to be fatally hit by a passing lorry.

Enter the woods by a gate and continue through the middle to emerge at a road by a signpost. Cross the road to a bridleway signpost and follow a good track till you come to a stile on your left. Cross this and walk south on a green track between two apple orchards, mature to the left, very young to the right, and reach a track going west through the orchard. Turn right along track then left following waymarks past a fishing lake and follow the perimeter to reach a concrete footpath signpost at the road from Twitty Fee. This unusual name is derived from the Twitye family which presumably held the property in fee. Turn left along this road (very little traffic) and, after passing Garlands Farm, turn left down Runsell Green back to the Anchor.

12 **Hatfield Peverel**
The Wheatsheaf

Hatfield Peverel is another Essex village which was originally on the main London to Colchester road and now enjoys a more peaceful existence thanks to the construction of a bypass many years ago. The real charm of Hatfield Peverel is its surroundings. To the north-west, beyond the railway, is Lord Rayleigh's Terling estate with its meadow and arable lands, fine trees and groups of farm buildings. To the south and south-west the land also has a wealth of trees and includes the grounds of Hatfield Priory. There are fine views of this land sloping gently down to the valley of the river Ter. South of the river the ground rises more steeply to the Nounsley ridge, with the high land of Little Baddow and Danbury beyond.

The Wheatsheaf is a friendly little pub with a bar decorated in the playing strips and scarfs of Newcastle United football club. The licensee is clearly a fan! Ridleys is the owner, and well cared for IPA Bitter and the newer ESX are on draught as well as Guinness and Strongbow cider. A good range of pub meals

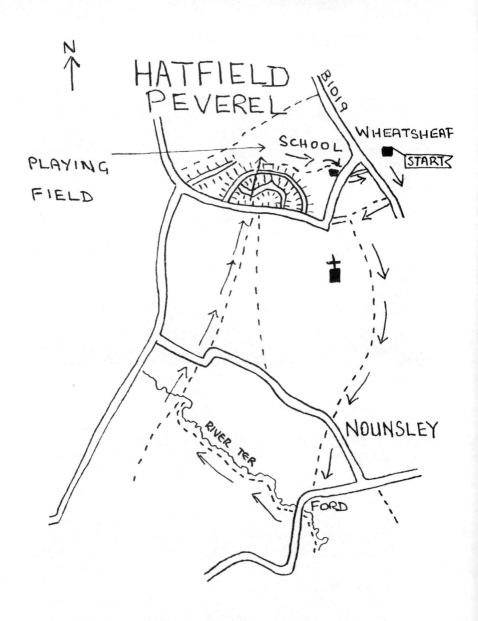

NOT TO SCALE.

is available in the restaurant, where children are welcome. In a neat little garden at the rear you can share the company of a cage of chipmunks.
Telephone: 0245 380330.

How to get there: Leave the A12 for Hatfield Peverel and from the Street join the B1019 signposted to Maldon. The Wheatsheaf is ¾ mile on the left.

Parking: Park at the pub but please ask for permission to leave your car before setting out on your walk.

Length of the walk: 2½ miles. Map: OS Landranger 167 Chelmsford and Harlow (inn GR 799114).

Though close to the village of Hatfield Peverel, this walk has views over the Chelmer valley, with a pleasant section along the river Ter. The route includes a wide circle round the church, part of a Benedictine monastery built in Norman times.

The Walk
Turn left outside the Wheatsheaf. At a road junction follow the road signposted towards Ulting. At the footpath sign before the Cross Keys pub turn right on a path which soon emerges at allotments. After 100 yards turn left and pass a burial ground. Over on the right is St Andrew's church which includes the nave of a Benedictine priory.

The priory started life as a college of secular canons dedicated to St Mary Magdalene and founded by Ingelrica, wife of Ranulph Peverel, in the reign of William II. Ingelrica's son William Peverel converted the foundation into a Benedictine priory which continued until the dissolution of the monasteries in 1537. Hatfield Priory, a Palladian mansion built in 1768, takes its name from this religious institution.

The path goes round the garden of a house and follows a fence out to the road beside the Sportmans Arms at Nounsley. Cross straight over the road to a path which soon comes to another road. Turn right and go downhill to cross the ford over the river Ter. Turn right by a footpath sign and follow the river bank upstream. Here the river is within a mile of joining the

St Andrew's church.

Chelmer. After five minutes you come to a weir and continue on to reach a long bridge over the river. Cross this and go uphill to a road. Walk up this for 100 yards and leave at a footpath sign in the same direction. When you come to a house follow along the side to a road. Cross straight over and walk on a path between two houses. Cross the first road and continue along the path. At the next road turn right and then left along Laburnum Way. Soon turn right between a fence and duck-pond through bushes to a playing field. Turn right along the edge of the playing field towards a school in the corner. There is a path at the left corner of the school which you follow to the road. Across the road to the left there is an unsigned track which runs north-east and soon leads you back to the Maldon Road opposite the Wheatsheaf.

13 Great Totham
The Bull

The cottages of Great Totham range along a group of roads at the foot of Beacon Hill and the island of Osea, which belongs to the parish, lies out in the Blackwater estuary. It was given by William the Conqueror to his nephew in 1066. In 1903 the island was purchased by Frederick Charrington to develop it as a seaside and health resort, and also as a temperance colony. A very fine prospectus was produced with excellent photographs promoting the idea of buying plots to build substantial houses on Osea. Included in this were artists's impressions of the type of houses Charrington wanted. He even bought a steamer, *Annie*, to sail from Maldon to Osea with visitors.

The Bull is a former Ind Coope house, standing in a prominent position at the bend of the road between Maldon and Colchester. 'Open all day' it proclaims, meaning 11 am to 11 pm, Monday to Saturday, and 12 noon to 3 pm, 7 pm to 10.30 pm on Sunday. The beers on draught are Tetley and Charrington IPA and there is Red Rock cider. There are two

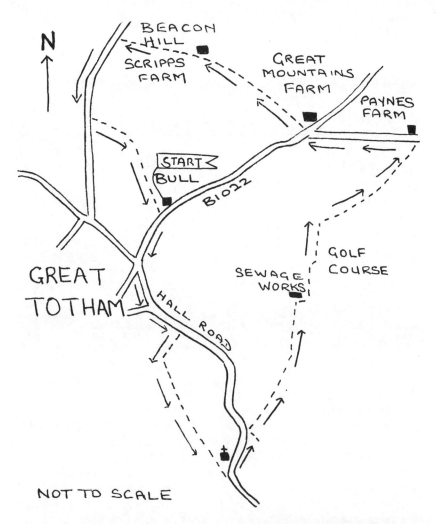

N

BEACON HILL
SCRIPPS FARM
GREAT MOUNTAINS FARM
PAYNES FARM

START
BULL

B1022

GREAT
TOTHAM

HALL ROAD

SEWAGE WORKS

GOLF COURSE

NOT TO SCALE

separate bars, and behind the lounge bar is a restaurant which welcomes families with children. In addition, a large garden may suit when the weather is fine. A wide selection of snacks and cooked food is available. I was drawn to the giant Yorkshire puddings with a great variety of fillings. Big appetites will certainly be satisfied by the Sunday roast or the intriguing 'busters'.

Telephone: 0621 891162.

How to get there: The B1022 is a pleasant route between Maldon and Colchester. About 2½ miles from the Maldon end is what may be described as Great Totham (south) and on this section, at a sharp bend, lies the Bull.

Parking: Park at the pub but please ask the landlord before leaving your car to go on the walk.

Length of the walk: 3 miles. Map: OS Landranger 168 Colchester and the Blackwater (inn GR 859119).

In the course of this walk there are many fine views of the Blackwater estuary and the land surrounding it – not to mention Osea Island and Northey Island. Standing on Beacon Hill you will get a fine idea of the layout of this area.

The Walk

Leaving the pub, cross carefully over the road, turning right to walk along the pavement to the post office. Turn left down Hall Road. Just after the last house on the right, turn right through a gateway and walk along a track for 80 yards to join a footpath. Turn left and pass a very large pond usually full of ducks. The path leads to St Peter's, the parish church of Great Totham. The church is largely 14th and 15th century. The original building, however, existed before 1222 and was left to the nuns of Clerkenwell. Not long ago a tastefully designed extension was added to the end of the church building. When passing one Sunday with a group of ramblers, I was invited to join the assembly for lunch! The records show that in the time of James I, a John Newton was in trouble with the archdeacon here for persistently refusing to sit in any pew save those where gentlewomen sat!

Pass through the churchyard – a charming spot – and turn left through the gate. A few yards up the road when it bends to the left take the footpath across a field which continues in the direction you have been walking. Cross a hedge and a small field going due north slightly to the left. You enter a thicket and walk right and left round a water treatment plant, then cross a bridge to emerge on a golf course. Follow a hedge to the left till you see a direction board.

St Peter's church lych gate, Great Totham.

At this point turn right and cross the golf course walking over three fairways with great caution. There are yellow waymarks to help with your sense of direction and footpath signs to lead you to a stile which marks your exit from the club. Continue between two fences to a road. Here turn left and walk (west) past two farms to the main road. A few yards to the left cross the road and join a footpath which climbs past Scripps Farm nearly to the top of Beacon Hill. When you reach the road, turn left downhill for 400 yards. At a footpath sign turn left for a delightful walk back down to the Bull.

14 Feering
The Bell Inn

Feering village, its Saxon name meaning 'the village by the Roman road', is a favourite of many, blessed by a happy grouping of buildings at a minor road junction. The 700-year-old church has Tudor brickwork of a very high standard and even the initials of Queen Elizabeth I scratched on to a 600-year-old glass window. Inside the church is a treasure – a rare Constable painting, unusually for him on a sacred subject (The Ascension), painted for the church at Manningtree, and later transferred to Feering. In 1814, Constable stayed at Feering and did a number of sketches of the village and the church.

In a lovely setting near the church you will find the Bell, a 14th century inn of character, offering ales and food for your sustenance and pleasure. As a Gray's house, the Bell serves Greene King IPA and Abbot Ale and also a guest beer which is changed every two or three months. The restaurant welcomes accompanied under 14s for food and (non-alcoholic) drink. There is also a separate games room for those who want a game

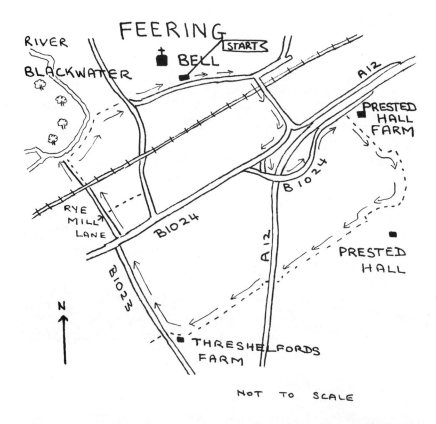

of pool or darts. The menu is full of options for snacks and tempting main dishes. A previous chef has left a legacy – the recipe for kleftiko, a tasty Greek dish of lamb and veal, which is a popular choice of the more adventurous.

Opening hours are from 11 am to 2.30 pm and 6 pm to 11 pm Monday to Saturday, 12 noon to 3 pm and 7 pm to 10.30 pm on Sunday.

Telephone: 0376 570375.

How to get there: Leave the A12 for Kelvedon if you are driving north-east and continue through the village. Feering is signposted about ½ mile after crossing the river bridge. Coming from the north-east follow the signs to Kelvedon and soon pick up the signs to Feering village.

68

Parking: At the pub, but please ask before setting out on the walk. Some street parking is also available.

Length of the walk: 3 miles. Map: OS Landranger 168 Colchester and the Blackwater (inn GR 872203).

An ancient and modern walk around the Feering parish, crossing on the way, over and under the London–Colchester railway line and also twice over the busy A12 roadway, by bridges. In other places there are many tranquil moments as you pass Prested Hall and Threshelfords Farm, and above all on the walk by the River Blackwater to Feering church, where only the bird calls may disturb the peace.

The Walk

Outside the Bell turn left along the lane. After 350 yards climb up right over the railway bridge and continue past a row of houses. At the T-junction turn right for a further 300 yards. Now turn left on a road signposted to Prested Hall, crossing the bridge over the A12. Follow the East Anglian Farm Ride sign along a concrete track behind some houses leading to Prested

The church, Feering.

Hall Farm. Turn right down a wide green track which runs along a hedge. At the end of the field turn right (west) and later pass the entrance to Prested Hall. Some 600 yards further along this track, you cross another bridge over the A12. Continue along this track till you reach the fence at Threshelfords Farm. At this point the path has been diverted to the right through a gap in the hedge and half-left to a path between a fence and a hedge out to the road. 'Footpath' signs are in place to mark this diversion. At the road turn right and cross the main road to walk up Rye Mill Lane. After walking under the railway line and just before the river Blackwater, turn right and walk upstream for the glorious last 600 yards of this walk as you climb out of the river scene through a gate to Feering village.

15 Canewdon
The Anchor

Here, at the top of Beacon Hill south of the river Crouch, was the command post in 1016 for Canute's decisive battle at nearby Ashingdon, overcoming the English king Edmund Ironside and by establishing a Dane on the throne, ending the centuries-old struggle with the Danes. The church (nearly 600 years old) occupies the top of the hill and is architecturally the finest in the Crouch valley, with a splendid tower which provides a reference point for miles around. The tower is 75 ft tall, with walls 7 ft thick, and it is made of ragstone which was probably brought by water from the Medway. Three heraldic shields are above the door; the middle shield shows the arms of France and England in Henry V's time, and another the arms of the Bohuns – Mary de Bohun was the king's mother. If you climb the hundred steps inside the tower, you are rewarded with the view of many square miles of Essex laid out before you, plus yachts off Burnham, ships rounding the Maplin sands and a sight of the Kent hills stretching up to meet the sky.

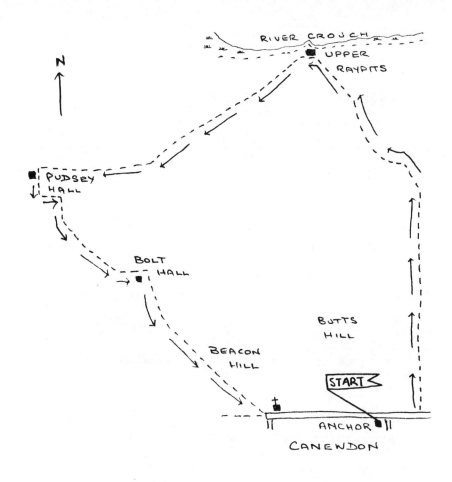

NOT TO SCALE.

The Anchor is a cosy pub with a grand open fire in one bar and two gas fires in the other. The building is 500 years old and the warm welcome has also something to do with the low-beamed ceilings. Real ales available are Tolly Cobbold, Tetley and Flowers, and Dry Blackthorn is on if you like cider. A custom-built children's room is immediately inside the door from the car park. The menu gives a full description of the wide variety of food on offer. My fancy was for Malaysian chicken,

chicken in a curry mayonnaise sauce topped with crisp salad, or you may prefer a 'Canewdon Buster', a giant spicy sausage in a roll with side salad; many more substantial dishes can also be ordered. Outside there is a patio with picnic tables, and an enclosed garden with swings and climbing things. Due to its geographical location, Canewdon is a very peaceful and isolated village. It's hard to believe that 900 years ago the history of England was changed here.

Telephone: 0702 258213.

How to get there: Travel east from Battlesbridge off the A130 or north from Rochford to Ashingdon; the road sign will tell you when to head east for Canewdon. When you reach the village proceed along Anchor Lane. Spot a High Street sign and you have arrived at the Anchor.

Parking: At the pub, but please let the landlord know before leaving your car to go on the walk.

Length of the walk: 3¼ miles. Map: OS Landranger 168 Colchester and the Blackwater (inn GR 901945).

All directions from Canewdon are downhill, so the walk has to end with a climb! Views open up of the boats and bustle of Burnham-on-Crouch and of the village of Althorne as you approach the river Crouch. The route then follows farmland before the exhilarating climb back to Canewdon.

The Walk
From the pub turn right down the High Street for 80 yards. At a footpath sign turn left down Gays Lane and descend Butts Hill. In about ½ mile you reach and cross a plank bridge and a stile. Turn left following the stream to a gatepost. As you approach the house at Upper Raypits, locate and cross the stile in the fence. Turn left past the house for ten yards then cross a stile on your left and walk in a pasture field. Cross a stile in the middle of the field and another stile out to the farm road. Cross the ditch on the road and another stile with a waymark. Walk diagonally over a field where tractor lines have been made, arriving at a hedge end. Follow the hedge right into the next field and to a marker post with yellow arrows on it. Turn left

The restored village lock-up, Canewdon

and cross the plank bridge walking to a fence post with yellow arrows. Turn left across the field for 100 yards, then half-right aiming for a protruding hedge corner. Continue in this direction to a fence leading left to Bolt Hall Farm. Follow the waymarks crossing the concrete track. Turn right round the back of the barn and cross another farm road. Cross diagonally the next small field and again cross a farm road. From here follow the rough path aiming directly for the church as you climb to the top of Beacon Hill. Now walk through the churchyard and past the lock-up and stocks (still being used in the middle of the last century, it is said) for a contented stroll down the High Street to the Anchor.

16 Steeple
The Sun and Anchor

Steeple, not to be confused with Steeple Bumpstead in the north of the county near the Suffolk border, is one of those unpretentious villages (just two pubs, three farms, a tea shop and a scattering of houses) in the Dengie peninsula which is a favourite for those, like me, who are attracted to this remote area between the Blackwater and the Crouch to the east of Maldon. Steeple probably gets its name because, due to sparseness of woodland hereabouts, and the lack of high buildings, the church tower is clearly visible for miles around. Though mainly flat, the land has some little hills between Mayland and Tillingham affording magnificent views of the estuary, which is in places 2 miles wide. On a clear day you can see beyond to Tollesbury and Great Totham. The overall impression is one of peace and tranquillity.

The Sun and Anchor is another Gray's house, unique to Essex, with careful thought given to the development of the property. In this case extensive land is included to the rear

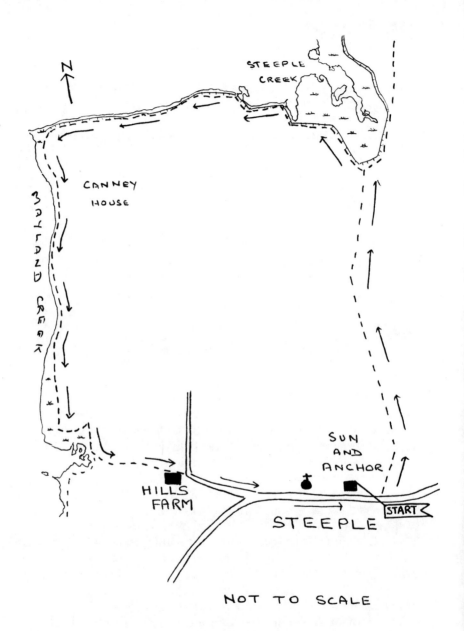

N

STEEPLE CREEK

CANNEY HOUSE

MAYLAND CREEK

HILLS FARM

SUN AND ANCHOR

START

STEEPLE

NOT TO SCALE

which in the past has been a campsite. More recently there have been occasional boot sales, and on one occasion mass car parking was provided one Saturday for a staging post of a St Peters Way walk by the Ramblers' Association. Real ales are Greene King IPA and Abbot plus guest beers, all dispensed by gravity. For cider lovers there is Red Rock. A good selection of food is served at lunchtimes and in the evening; among the choices are steaks, scampi, cod, lasagne and gammon. Bar snacks include sandwiches, and sausages and chips. There is a games room with pool and darts and a fine children's room where the family may eat. On fine days an extensive garden provides an alternative venue for pleasant eating and drinking.

Opening hours are from 11 am to 3 pm and 6 pm to 11 pm on Mondays to Saturdays (12 noon to 3 pm and 7 pm to 10.30 pm Sundays).

Telephone: 0621 772700.

How to get there: From Latchingdon the road to Steeple is signposted at the mini-roundabout. The Sun and Anchor is in the centre of the village just past the church.

Parking: You can park at the pub but please ask the landlord before setting out on your walk.

Length of the walk: 3¾ miles. Map: OS Landranger 168 Colchester and the Blackwater (inn GR 937029).

The walk takes a direct route to the sea wall at Steeple Creek, with Osea Island always in sight. The island can be reached only by boat from the Dengie, or via a causeway from the other side of the estuary at low tide. The route follows the sea wall before travelling up Mayland Creek, which is full of interest, such as birds, boats and big skies. The last stretch is across farmland with the church steeple of Steeple beckoning you back.

The Walk
As you leave the pub turn left along the pavement and immediately you will see a concrete footpath post pointing north between two fences. Walk this way and through some scrub. After a few yards bear right and climb over two metal stiles at a derelict old cottage. Turn left between the cottage and

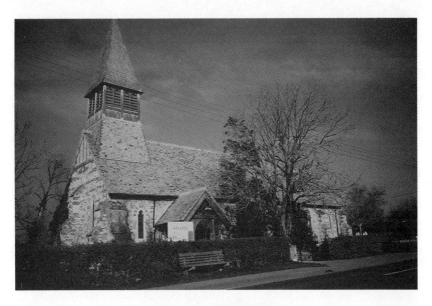

St Laurence church, Steeple.

more scrub and then follow a path right and left to another
metal stile. There is a playing-field to your right. Having crossed
yet another stile a good path goes straight on between two
crops for 700 yards. Cross a bridge to the right-hand side of the
ditch and continue past a thicket on your left bearing right still
with a hedge on your left to the sea wall. Climb up and turn left
on top of the wall. What a fine view of Osea Island is before
you! Now walk to Canney House, all along the side of the wide
estuary. Canney House lies remotely at the end of Mayland
Creek but now has the company of weekend and summer
houses, as well as providing a haven for many boats. Past the
boat yard the path becomes rougher, going south by Mayland
Creek. After ¾ mile turn left with the path and then right
towards the creek. Cross a metal stile and head inland with a
fence on your left. Follow the fence round to your left and walk
to the buildings at Hill's Farm. Here are two gates to negotiate
before walking between barns past a large pond and then the
farmhouse to the farm road leading to the Maldon Road. Keep
going towards the church steeple and just past it you arrive at
the Sun and Anchor.

17 Layer Breton
The Hare and Hounds

Between Abberton Reservoir and Colchester there lies an area of Essex largely unaffected by recent times and remarkably peaceful. I am referring to Layer Breton, Birch Green and Birch. Perhaps more surprising is the startling magnificence of Layer Marney Towers, an eight-storey building dating back to Tudor times, and yet only intended as the gatehouse to a home for Sir Henry Marney, Privy Counsellor to Henry VII. Completion was overtaken when Sir Henry died leaving no descendants. Of course a visit to the Towers is a must – either in the course of your walk or, if this is not possible, on another occasion. If you climb to the eighth floor you will be rewarded by the sight of a wonderful painting.

Also built in the sixteenth century is the nearby Hare and Hounds public house at Birch Green on the northern edge of Layer Breton. This is a very attractive little pub but beware of Gertie, a ghost who is reputed always to be around and sometimes to make her presence apparent. The Hare and

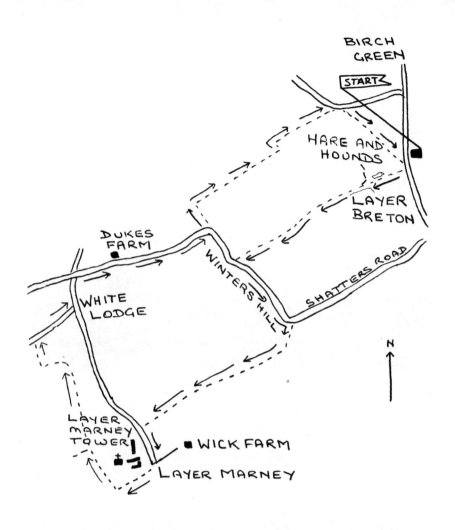

BIRCH
GREEN

START

HARE AND
HOUNDS

LAYER
BRETON

DUKES
FARM

WINTERS HILL

SHATTERS ROAD

WHITE
LODGE

N

LAYER
MARNEY
TOWER

WICK FARM

LAYER MARNEY

NOT TO SCALE

Hounds is now a freehouse and boasts a children's room and a large car park, as well as a good garden. The room and the garden have various games and diversions for the young, including a small snooker table, swings and a slide. For the grown-ups the real ales available are Adnams, Tetley and Greene King IPA. Scrumpy Jack cider is on tap. A roast meal is served at lunchtime on Sundays. At other times the food is traditional pub fare – sandwiches, ploughman's and dishes of scampi, gammon and lamb. Opening hours are from 12 noon to 2.30 pm and 6.30 pm to 11 pm Mondays to Saturdays, and 12 noon to 3 pm, 7 pm to 10.30 pm Sundays.

Telephone: 0206 330249.

How to get there: Layer Breton is on an unnumbered 3 mile road just south of Birch which connects the B1026 to the B1022.

Parking: The pub has a spacious car park, but please mention to the landlord when you are leaving for the walk.

Length of the walk: 3½ miles. Map: OS Landranger 168 Colchester and the Blackwater (inn GR 943188).

The highlight of this walk is the spectacular Marney Towers which, if you have time, is well worth a visit. The route takes you through peaceful countryside where you may see domesticated deer and several varieties of sheep. All the Layers (Layer de la Haye, Layer Marney and Layer Breton) derive their name from the little Layer brook. Nowadays it disappears into Abberton Reservoir.

The Walk

From the pub cross the green and the main road to a concrete footpath sign. Follow a farm track, passing ducks and geese. Keep straight on between a hedge and a pond to cross a stile into a field. Follow the good headland path at the side of the hedge for nearly ½ mile to a narrow country road. On the way there are extensive views to your left over Abberton Reservoir and to Great Wigborough church. Turn left down the lane (Winters Hill) and when the road turns sharply to the left turn right up a hedged footpath. Follow the waymark by the hedge when you reach a field and keep along this hedge till it turns to the right. Now continue your direction straight across the field following the direction of the yellow arrow. The farmer has left a wide path through the crop.

On reaching the road at a concrete footpath sign turn left downhill. Turn right to pass Marney Towers in all its glory. The architect was Girolamo de Travizi and he certainly produced

Layer Marney Towers.

one of the most amazing sights in Essex. Made of brick and terracotta, the gatehouse is 80 ft high, with two turrets of eight storeys framing two huge windows above a huge doorway. The parapets are richly decorated, and the chimneys are a fitting crown to this marvellous place.

Sir Henry Marney was nearly the end of a line dating from Norman times – his son died a year after him and there were no heirs. In the family chapel within the adjacent Layer Marney church, the tombs of Sir Henry and his son, John, lie together beside that of William Marney who died in 1360. Carved leopards and shields with Marney badges surround the tombs. Layer Marney Tower, together with the adjoining rare breed animals and deer park, is open every day except Saturday from April to early October from 2 pm to 6 pm. Telephone 0206 330784 for more details. At the time of writing admission prices were £3 for adults, £1.50 for children and £8 for a family.

After passing the front of the church go right and again right past the back of the church. You will probably see here a herd of domesticated deer and various breed of sheep. The path comes to a junction – take the ongoing path signposted to

Smythes Green. At the top of the hill, turn left and right through the hedge. Then go left (west) for 130 yards to a telegraph pole. Now turn right across the field to pass a pond on your right and reach a concrete footpath sign at a road. Here turn right. At the junction near White Lodge turn left, and then right past Dukes, an impressive looking house by a farm. When the road bends sharply to the right, turn left at a concrete footpath sign. Now follow a track for more than ½ mile. Just as the track reaches a road turn right at another concrete footpath sign, and walk down a pretty lane behind houses to reach the heath by the Hare and Hounds.

18 Burnham-on-Crouch
The Star Inn

Burnham is the leading sailing base on the east side of England, and you will probably quickly tire of trying to count the number of craft on the river. The High Street abounds with pubs, restaurants and shops and is characterised by the mid-Victorian clock tower. For the non-sailors, riverside walking is a popular pursuit.

There are several licensed establishments in and around Burnham. The Star, which is a freehouse, is certainly one which appears to be prospering, as it deserves to. Opening hours are from 11 am to 11 pm Monday to Saturday and 12 noon to 3 pm and 7 pm to 10.30 pm on Sunday. It is the only pub in Burnham which fronts on to the High Street and has a rear entrance from the sea wall. The real ales are frequently changed, though often there are Adnams, Crouch Vale Woodham and Eldridge Pope. Olde English cider is on tap. Many sorts of food are available; when I was there, among the home-cooked items taking the eye were, beef and mushroom pie and seafood lasagne. A few years

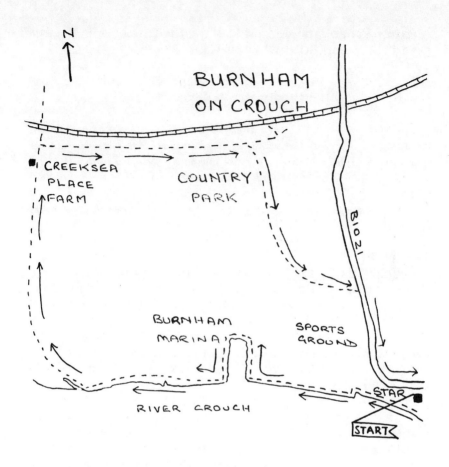

NOT TO SCALE

ago a family room was added, with a pool table. Residential accommodation is also available. Apparently there is a supernatural presence in the building which hides valuables for weeks on end only to return them to an obscure place. If you do stay here it may be better to keep your rings on!

Telephone: 0621 782010.

How to get there: Whether travelling from Maldon or South Woodham Ferrers, make for Latchingdon. The B1010 is your road from there to Burnham. The Star Inn is on the right.

Parking: Park on the south side of the High Street or in the free car park up Ship Road which is signposted.

Length of the walk: 2¾ miles. Map: OS Landranger 168 Colchester and the Blackwater (GR 951956).

The walk goes up river, then around the marina, which was constructed some years ago against the wishes of the Ramblers' Association and many local residents. One consolation for this severance in the sea wall is the view at close hand of some of the craft berthed in Burnham. The walk continues by the river to Creeksea where after a little climb you head north for just ½ mile to the railway. Another path going east returns us through the country park and so back to the town.

The Walk

Leave the Star by the back door and thread your way through the patio tables to the walkway by the sea wall. Turn right along the quay past an assortment of teashops, seafood bars, boat builders and, later, houseboats. The river is over 400 yards wide at this point. In smuggling days many contraband cargoes were run into the Crouch, mainly from the Low Countries and Dunkirk. About 1730, Dick Turpin was known as a smuggler in the Dengie Hundred.

Soon you come to the marina, which you must walk round in order to progress up river. A third of a mile beyond the marina the path swings to the right and climbs inland to Creeksea Place Farm. As you come to the railway line turn right along a terraced path walking east with the river ½ mile down to your right. Cross the access road to the marina. You are now in Burnham Country Park. Turn to your right and aim for the far corner between houses on the left and caravans to the right. You arrive at a stream crossing near some rugby pitches. Turn left past the pitches and right towards a sports centre. On your left the road leads to the main road (Station Road). Turn right downhill and soon you will be back at the Star.

With the abundance of outdoor life to look at it is easy to forget the fine church, which, in true Essex fashion, is a mile from the centre of town. The lord of the manor regarded the church as his personal province, so he put it next to him. This church belonged to Dunmow Priory from the 12th century to

Burnham marina.

the Dissolution, which perhaps accounts for its splendour. The seven great windows facing the churchyard are impressive. Two monstrous grotesques are at the corner of the porch, and a medieval scratch dial is on a buttress. The font, the oldest feature, is a square Norman bowl.

A very early industry carried on in the neighbourhood was the recovery of salt from sea water, drawn from shallow tanks cut out in the marshes and filled by high tides. Evaporation took place in pans of lead or earthenware over trenches in which wood fires were laid. The soil, removed in the cutting out of these tanks and trenches, accounts for the mounds known as Red Hills and largely composed of burnt earth, now standing on the marshes. 'Wick' or 'wich' denoted a place connected with the production of salt.

If you have time, why not visit Ewenny Alternative Environment Centre (off the B1020 in Southminster) or the Mangapps Farm Railway Museum (steam railways) on the B1021 just before you reach Burnham.

19 Dedham
The Sun Hotel

Dedham is a town close to the border with Suffolk and made famous by John Constable's paintings of the Stour valley. For its size it can stand comparison with any in the country. The church, whose tower is possibly the most familiar of all Essex architectural sights, is nearly 500 years old and its magnificence reflects the prosperity of the wool trade from 1400 to 1700. The building stands in the middle of Dedham and from virtually any point in the town the church is visible, watching like a shepherd over the parish. It was finished in 1520, and so constructed that a carriage could pass beneath the tower, which is 130 ft high.

Once a Saxon settlement and then a Norman manor, Dedham was granted a fair by the king's chancellor in the reign of Richard II and this stimulated the trade in cloth, some of the profits from which were converted into distinguished buildings along the High Street. The best of the old buildings in the High Street is the Sun Hotel, opposite the church, where our excursion begins.

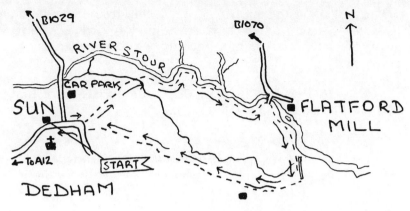

NOT TO SCALE

This is a splendid old building, parts of which are 500 years old. The Sun was a coaching inn, and to this day offers overnight accommodation which I can personally recommend. On the ground floor is the bar with a large adjoining room where children are welcome and there is a good garden at the back behind the car park. Real ales served are Adnams and John Smith's plus one guest beer. The tap cider is Strongbow. A wide range of excellent food is available ranging from snacks such as jacket potatoes to substantial meals like steak and kidney pie. The Sun is open all day Monday to Saturday in the summer, while in the winter it is shut between 2.30 pm and 6 pm. Sunday hours are 12 noon to 3 pm and 7 pm to 10.30 pm.

The Sun saw the last person to be burned as a witch in England. She was called Elsa, and this ceremony took place in the Sun's back garden. From time to time, so it is said, her ghost returns to visit the premises.

Telephone: 0206 323351.

How to get there: Leave the A12 when you see the signs to Stratford St Mary and Dedham, on to the B1029. As you near the A12 again turn right over the main road and drive into Dedham High Street. Turn left into the Sun Hotel car park opposite the church.

Parking: Park at the Sun Hotel, or on the street from October to March. There is a free car park within 400 yards. If you park at the Sun please ask behind the bar before you start on your walk.

Length of the walk: 3 miles. Map: OS Landranger 168 Colchester and the Blackwater (inn GR 057332).

To walk from Dedham to Flatford Mill and back by Lower Barn Farm, is to pass through the pages of history. Part of the route is along the banks of the river Stour to the mill that so inspired Constable, passing an automatic lock and a weir on the return journey.

The Walk
Outside the Sun Hotel turn left and follow the main street for 250 yards. When the road bears at right angles to the right, discover a concrete footpath sign and follow the track to the north-east. Cross a stile near Dedham Hall Farm and bear right to another stile after which you walk along a fenced track. Cross the old river which is the county boundary and keep on to another stile close by the river Stour. From here you follow the river bank passing the Fen Bridge and walking all the way to a stile by a bridge near Flatford Mill.

Near the footbridge is the picturesque thatched cottage depicted in Constable's *View of the Stour*. It is well worth crossing the bridge for a closer look at Flatford Mill itself, a large red-brick house with dormer windows and part weatherboarded. Also, there is the white farmhouse called Willie Lotts Cottage featured in many of Constable's finest paintings. You may stop here for refreshments and browse around the shops though it can be a busy spot in the summer months, especially at the weekends.

Always noted for his penmanship but not sufficiently academic to take religious orders, John Constable (1776–1837) first exhibited at the Royal Academy in 1802. There was little notice taken of his paintings at home, though they were well received in Paris and Lille in 1825. He also had a long wait for marriage to the lady he loved, and, sadly, after 12 years of happy wedlock she died. After Constable's death his paintings fetched ten times the price they did whilst he was alive. He was

Flatford Mill.

elected a member of the Royal Academy at the belated age of 53.

Cross back over the bridge when you are ready and turn left along the right bank of the river, passing an interesting automatic lock and soon the famous scene of Constable's Flatford Mill presents itself.

The walk continues to the weir and you walk over this to a stile on the right. Cross this and soon reach a gate and a stile. This you also cross and continue along a grass track to a concrete farm road. Turn right and follow this road round bends. Just past a thicket on your left when the road turns sharp left, go straight on over a stile. The path crosses a field and then follows a fence on your right. When you reach a thicket on your right the path crosses the middle of the field on your left to a stile in the hedge opposite. Now continue by a well-defined path to a stile and onwards out to the road. Turn right, and left at the corner retracing your steps back to the Sun Hotel.

20 **Great Bentley**
The Royal Fusilier

Here we find a village green of 42 acres, claimed to be the largest in Britain, where since Norman times children have played their games. Certainly its spaciousness is impressive.

The Royal Fusiler is at nearby Aingers Green and its name may echo the military connections of not so far away Colchester. This little pub was extended a few years ago to include two bars, a games room, a children's room and a patio. The original building is 200 years old, and the present owner has presided for many of the more recent of these over this neat and friendly freehouse. The real ales are Adnams and one guest beer, while cider lovers can have Scrumpy Jack. The Royal Fusiler does not provide full meals, but freshly made sandwiches are available. This is a pub in which trade is largely local but where readers of this book will be made welcome.

Opening hours are from 11 am to 3 pm and 6 pm to 11 pm Mondays to Saturdays, 12 noon to 3 pm and 7 pm to 10.30 pm Sundays.

Telephone: 0206 250001.

How to get there: The A1200 is the trunk road connecting the A12 eastwards to Harwich and Clacton. Leave this road on the A133 signposted to Weeley and Clacton. A minor road leaves the A133 going south to Great Bentley. When you reach the principal road at the massive green turn right and left past the Plough pub over the level crossing. In ½ mile, after reaching Aingers Green, turn left along Weeley road to reach the Royal Fusilier.

Parking: Park behind the pub but please ask the landlord before setting out on your walk.

Length of the walk: 3½ miles. Map: OS Landranger 168 Colchester and the Blackwater (inn GR 119204).

The walk starts from the pub in Aingers Green, which is about ½ mile from Great Bentley railway station. A crossfield path brings you to the edge of the huge green at Great Bentley, passing some 400-year-old houses on the way to the yet more ancient church with its 600-year-old tower, and other parts dating back to the year 1100. By another field path we come to a level crossing and then to the farm by the site of Frating Abbey. You return via a quiet lane, a field path, a wood and a track.

The Walk

Leave the pub and turn right to the crossroads. Turn right again (the road is signposted to Tendring). After 300 yards turn left off the road by a black footpath sign. The line of the path has been marked by tractor wheels. Follow this turning right on the way to a crossing farm road. Turn left on this to reach a road near the railway station. Turn right and cross the level crossing to come to the edge of the great green. Walk between the pond and some interesting houses (Palfreymans House and the Old Rectory) to come to St Mary's church. You pass two more pubs on the way – the Plough and the Red Lion.

The church stands proudly in a large churchyard. There is a 14th century timbered porch and a carved Norman doorway inside. It is worth noting how skilfully the carpenters used their tools to carve the chevrons, the sunflowers and other ornaments of the doorway which also has two medieval sundials on its other side. The chancel was lengthened and the solid tower

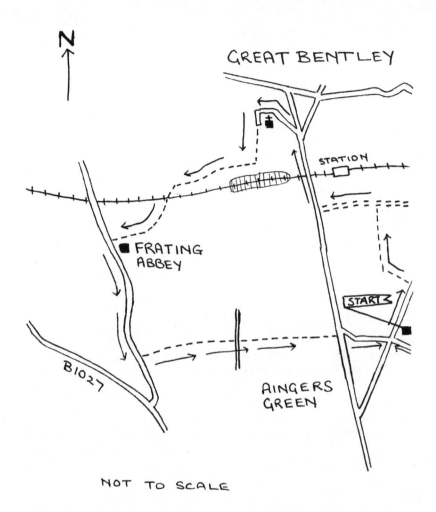

N

GREAT BENTLEY

STATION

FRATING
ABBEY

B1027

START

AINGERS
GREEN

NOT TO SCALE

added 600 years ago. More recently the roof of the chancel and
the nave were revealed, and they are splendid examples of
500-year-old timber work. The front was presented by Robert
de Vere, Earl of Oxford, in 1221. The stone spiral staircase still
remains. It once led up to the rood screen gallery.

The 16th century was an era of religious persecution in the
area, one vicar being deposed for marrying. His successor
denounced five parishioners for being Protestants and saw them
burned at the stake in Colchester. Three of the five were a

Palfreyman's house, Great Bentley.

20-year-old-girl and her parents. Agents of the torturers met the girl and tried to shake her faith by putting her hand in a candle flame, but she declared that if she were made to burn she would be given the strength to bear it. All of this punishment was given for the 'crime' of reading the bible together. The 18th and 19th centuries were more tolerant in Great Bentley, when a Quaker house and a Methodist chapel were accepted. Members of both were still buried in the churchyard. In recent times Roman Catholics have regularly celebrated mass in the church.

In the churchyard a yellow arrow points to the right where a gate leads out to a farm track and on to a five-barred gate with another direction sign to the right. Walk the field edge round to an earth bridge and on to an opening in the railway embankment fence, which leads to a crossing. Take care as you cross. Now keep to the left side of the ditch ahead then soon cross an earth bridge to follow tractor lines to the track at the side of the field. Follow the track to the right through the farm buildings out to a lane. Turn left by a concrete footpath sign passing the site of Frating Abbey. Barely ½ mile down the lane turn left by a concrete footpath sign down the field to cross a small stream by a succession of three plank bridges. Cross a stile and climb the meadow to cross another stile. Walk to the left for a few yards and pick up a well-marked path on the right across the field heading a few yards to the left of a straw store with a corrugated roof. Pass along a track just inside the wood ahead. A track on the right side of the hedge ahead leads to Aingers Green. Cross the road and follow Weeley Road to the Royal Fusiler.